Arts & Crafts

WEAVING

Susie O'Reilly

With photographs by Zul Mukhida

Thomson Learning
New York

Frontispiece *A weaving from the Andes mountains in Bolivia, South America.*

First published in the
United States in 1993 by
Thomson Learning
115 Fifth Avenue
New York, NY 10003

First published in 1993 by
Wayland (Publishers) Ltd.

Cataloging-in-Publication Data applied for

ISBN: 1-56847-067-3

Printed in Italy

CONTENTS

Words printed in **bold** appear in the glossary

GETTING STARTED

Cloth is made from **fibers**. Some fibers, such as cotton and linen, come from plants. Others, such as wool, come from animals. Artificial fibers are made from **chemicals**. There are three main ways of putting fibers together to make a piece of cloth: **felting, knitting,** and weaving. In weaving, a piece of equipment called a loom is used. **Vertical** fibers (called the warp) are held tight on the loom while **horizontal** fibers (the weft) are **interlaced** through them to make a kind of **grid**.

With careful planning, fibers of different colors can be interlaced to make a piece of cloth that has a pattern or picture woven into it.

Weaving can be done by hand or by machine. This book is about different ways of hand weaving. It looks especially at **tapestry** weaving, which uses a very simple frame loom. Other methods of hand weaving use more complicated looms, which take more time to set up but enable the fibers to be woven into cloth more quickly.

▲ *This woolen tapestry was designed by schoolchildren.*

◀ *Scotland is famous for its thick woven cloth, called tweed. This woman is using a traditional hand loom to make tweed.*

In the eighteenth and nineteenth centuries, the **Industrial Revolution** brought great changes, first to Western Europe and then to the United States. Factories were built containing huge looms driven by steam and other kinds of power. Today, computers are used to design fabric and control looms. This way cloth can be made quickly and cheaply. However, many modern **textile** companies still employ hand weavers. These weavers develop ideas and try out new designs for cloth, which will then be woven in huge quantities by machine.

▲ *A weaving from Bolivia. Look how the shape of the horse has been woven into the pattern.*

SETTING UP YOUR WORK AREA

You will need to collect these tools and materials to get started.

Paper
A variety of different papers, both printed and plain
Cardboard boxes

Fibers
For the warp—strong, thin cotton string or button thread
For the weft—any long, straight fibers, for example: string, cotton thread, raffia, silk thread, woolen yarn, ribbons, strips of leather, wire, nylon thread, strips of cloth, cellophane

Found objects—collect objects to weave into your cloth, for example: feathers, beads, shells, bones, stones, metal washers, curtain rings, wood shavings, twigs, strips of bark, bottle tops, candy wrappers, seeds, dried grass, plant stalks, jewelry

To make looms
Look for: old picture frames, round cheese boxes, shoe boxes, wooden and cardboard vegetable boxes, door or window frames, bicycle wheels, lampshade frames, forked branches

General equipment
Scissors
A cutting board, ruler, and craft knife
Masking tape
Needles and a **bodkin**
A flat piece of wood to use as a **shuttle**
Velcro
Screw eyes
Poster paints
White glue
Cardboard for mounting
Cold-water dyes, salt, rubber gloves, a plastic bowl to use as a dye bath, and a wooden spoon
Plastic wrap
Colored pens or crayons
Tracing paper

WEAVING IN OTHER TIMES

Weaving is a very ancient craft, dating back at least 5,000 years. The very earliest cloth has not survived, but **archaeologists** have found very old stone and pottery **weights,** which were hung on the bottom of the warp threads to keep them **taut.**

We know that the **ancient Greeks** wove, because paintings on Greek vases sometimes show people weaving. Also, some Greek **legends** tell about weaving. For example there is a story about the goddess Athena and a woman called Arachne. The two had a competition to see who was the best weaver. Arachne won, so Athena turned her into a spider!

The oldest surviving piece of woven cloth was found in Egypt, in the tomb of the **Pharaoh** Thutmose IV. It is thought to have been made in 1500 B.C.

▲ *This ancient Greek vase is decorated with a painting of a very simple loom. It shows the stone weights used to hold the warp threads taut.*

Pieces of burial cloths from Peru, from the sixth century, have also been found and **preserved**. The Peruvians wove wonderful pictures of birds, such as eagles and vultures, into these cloths. Sometimes they would weave only a part of an animal or person—perhaps just a huge nose instead of a whole face, or a claw instead of a whole cat. They used one small part to suggest the whole creature.

◄ *A piece of tapestry woven in Peru about 1,500 years ago. It shows the head of a jaguar and two other jaguars standing back to back.*

Among the most skillful weavings ever made were tapestries woven in the **Middle Ages** in France and Flanders (a country which now forms parts of Belgium, the Netherlands, and France). They were hung on the walls of castles and palaces to decorate the rooms and keep out drafts. Kings took their tapestries with them when they traveled. Soldiers took them when they went to battle and hung them up in their tents.

In the nineteenth century, the English craftsman William Morris and his friend, Sir Edward Coley Burne-Jones, admired these medieval tapestries so much that they tried to discover how they had been made. They started a weaving company and wove some beautiful pieces that retold medieval legends.

▲ *Part of a tapestry woven in Germany in the fifteenth century. It shows an autumn scene.*

▼ *A tapestry designed by William Morris in the 1850s. The blue leaves were once green. The wool has faded over the years.*

LOOMS FROM AROUND THE WORLD

The weaver's main tool is the loom. Looms come in all shapes and sizes. Some are made of wood, some of metal. Some use few materials and are very simply made. Others are complicated and carefully **engineered.**

▲ *A weaver from Guatemala using a back-strap loom and (above right) an example of cloth.*

The back-strap loom makes good use of a simple idea. At one end, the warp threads are tied to a tree or the side of a house. The other ends are strapped around the hips of the weaver. The warps are kept taut by moving the body. This sort of loom is used in many countries (for example, Peru, Mexico, Guatemala, Thailand, Vietnam, and northern Japan) and very beautiful cloth can be woven.

A Bedouin woman from Qatar, in the Middle ▶ *East, preparing a horizontal ground loom.*

The **nomadic** Bedouin people in the Middle East do not live in permanent homes. They move from place to place with their herds, looking for grazing land. Because of this, they use simple, horizontal ground looms that can be pulled up and packed away when it is time to move on. The job of weaving is done by the women. They make cloth that is used for tents, sacks, saddle bags, cushions, and rugs.

The Navaho people in Arizona and New Mexico weave beautiful blankets and rugs using a strong, upright wooden frame loom. Sometimes two trees form the sides of the frame, but more often wooden poles are used.

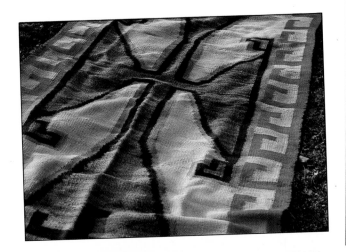

▲ A Navaho woman with her loom and (above left) a Navaho rug with a typical bold pattern.

◀ Weaving cotton in the Gambia, West Africa, on a loom worked by a foot treadle.

In West Africa, the men weave on light, narrow upright looms, which they work with their feet using a **treadle.** The cloth is made in strips, sometimes as narrow as five or six inches. The strips are sewn together to make wider pieces of cloth.

Today, most hand weavers in developed countries use tapestry looms or wooden-framed treadle looms. These are like the looms that were used to weave silk in China 2,000 years ago. They were used in Europe in the Middle Ages and by the first Europeans to settle in North America in the seventeenth century. Until the 1880s, many families in the United States wove their own cloth on a treadle loom.

WEAVING TODAY

Today, hand weavers in developed countries design and make decorative pieces to be used as wall hangings or rugs. Like all artists, weavers use a wide variety of **techniques**, materials, and ideas.

As in the past, many weavers today make tapestries that tell a story. The work of Ruth Scheuer reflects life in New York. Joanna Buxton, from England, has made a series of tapestries about famous women in history.

Most weavers are interested in exploring color and shape. Sharon Marcus, from the United States, uses the shapes of buildings in her tapestries. The work of the English weaver, Marta Rogoyska, contains huge **abstract** shapes, sometimes based on the patterns seen in rocks and crystals. Liza Collins, another English weaver, uses sea creatures and desert plants to inspire her work.

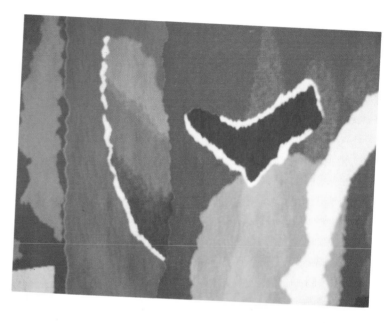

▲ *Detail of a wool tapestry by Marta Rogoyska. The design for this weaving was based on a collage of torn paper.*

▼ **Departure** *by Sharon Marcus. Think about the way color has been used in this weaving.*

◄ *A weaving by Liza Collins called* Growingscape.

For some weavers, it is the kind of materials used that matters. Polish-born Tadek Beutlich uses coarse, hairy rope and string. He enjoys the **three-dimensional texture** these fibers give his work. Other weavers prefer to work with finer, softer fibers, such as silk.

A wall hanging by Mary Restieaux. The silk warps were specially dyed before weaving began. ▶

▼ *Vibrations III, a tapestry by Tadek Beutlich. It uses sisal fibers, which are made from a plant grown in the West Indies.*

Cloth woven by people from other times and other cultures provides good ideas for today's weavers. For example, Mary Restieaux studied the cloth made in Uzbekistan, in Central Asia, in the nineteenth century. Then she developed work using the same technique of dyeing the silk warps before attaching them to the loom.

Many exciting pieces of modern weaving have been **commissioned** for particular places. One of the biggest weavings ever made was commissioned for the new Coventry Cathedral in England, rebuilt after World War II. The artist Graham Sutherland was asked to design a tapestry to hang above the altar. It is about 75 feet by 46 feet.

PAPER WEAVING

Weaving with strips of paper is a good introduction to weaving, because it can be done without a loom. With paper weaving, you can learn how to interlace separate strips.

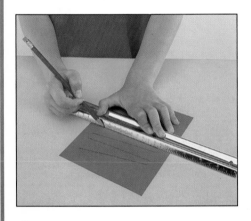

1 On a piece of paper, mark a series of lines, stopping well short of the edge.

2 Put the paper on a cutting board. Cut along the lines with a craft knife.

3 Cut several strips of paper of another color.

6 Continue weaving in strips until you have completely filled the piece of paper.

7 Make different patterns by cutting thicker and thinner strips of paper, and by weaving in the weft strips in different ways.

8 You can glue your weavings to thicker paper to make greeting cards and wall hangings, or combine several pieces to make a giant collage.

4 Take one of the strips. Weave it over and then under the cuts in the first piece of paper.

5 Take a second strip. This time weave it under and then over the cuts.

SETTING UP A TAPESTRY FRAME

Tapestry weavings are made using a frame loom. All sorts of everyday objects can be used as frames. For example, try a shoe box, a vegetable or fruit box, a forked branch, a lampshade frame, a bicycle wheel, a door, the legs of an upturned table, or a ladder.

The frame needs to be **rigid** and stable. A large frame can be used by several people working at once.

▲ *A circular weavng made using a hubcap.*

1 To warp up the frame, use strong, thin cotton string. Tie one end securely to one side of the frame.

2 Take the string to the opposite side and begin to wrap it around the frame in evenly spaced, **parallel lines.** It may help to cut notches in the frame to hold the warp in place.

3 When the frame is filled, cut the string and tie the end to the frame.

4 Now thread a piece of the same string *across* the frame, at the top of the warp threads. Tie it to the first warp and wind it around each of the warps in turn. Then tie it to the last warp. Do the same at the bottom. This helps to give a good surface for weaving.

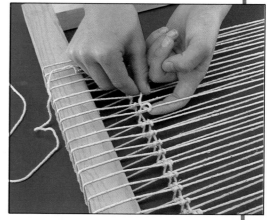

◀ *Examples of different frames (clockwise from top left): a vegetable crate; a forked tree branch; a drying rack; a hubcap; a picture frame.*

MAKING A TAPESTRY WEAVING

Tapestry weavings can be made in any size, large or small. You can make very tiny mats or enormous hangings. You can work alone or with others as a team.

1 Decide what you are going to make. If you are going to hang the finished piece in a particular place, make sure the size, design, and colors are suitable.

2 Make sketches of your design. Then draw up a full-sized color plan (see page 28). This plan is called a **cartoon**.

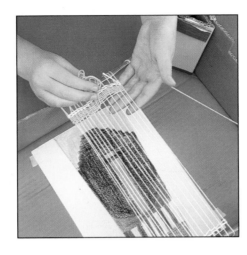

4 Now weave in the weft. Some people use a bodkin to do this. Others use a wooden shuttle. Choose whatever suits the job best. Often a length of thread rolled in a small ball, and your fingers, will be the easiest method.

3 Choose a suitable frame and make the warp (see page 15). Place the cartoon behind the warp and attach it with masking tape.

5 Push down each row of weft firmly with your fingers or a broad-toothed comb.

6 Do not pull the weft threads too tight. Try to keep an even **tension** so that the outer edges remain straight.

7 When you have finished, cut the warp threads off the loom. Tie them together using small, tidy knots. Either cut the spare string off, or leave it as a fringe.

8 Neatly sew in any loose ends of threads at the back of the weaving, using a tapestry needle.

9 To hang the work on the wall, sew a piece of Velcro along the top edge of the weaving. Cut a strip of wood the same width as your hanging and put a screw eye at either end. Thread through some picture cord. Glue the other half of the Velcro onto the wood. Attach the weaving with the Velcro.

FURTHER IDEAS

2 You can give your work a three-dimensional effect, or add extra details and decoration, by weaving in found objects. You can also try embroidering some areas of your weaving.

1 Fringe can be added in thread to match the warp or weft. Cut the thread into six-inch lengths. One at a time, fold each piece in half and push the folded end through the edge of the weaving. Pull the ends through the loop to make a double hitch knot.

▲ *A double hitch knot.*

TURN TO PAGES 28-29 FOR INSTRUCTIONS ON WEAVING COLOR PATTERNS INTO YOUR TAPESTRY.

PROJECTS USING CARDBOARD

MAKING A PAINTED HANGING

1 Find a large old cardboard box (or two small ones). Open it up and lay it out flat.

2 Paint a bold design or picture on the box with poster paints thickened with white glue.

3 When the paint is dry, cut the cardboard into strips, using a craft knife and a ruler.

Remember: Take great care when using a knife. Use a cutting board. Ask an adult to help.

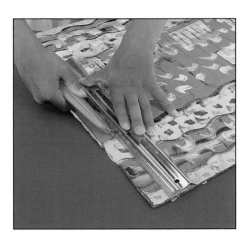

4 Use some of the strips as the warp and some as the weft. Weave them together to form a new painting.

5 Mount your picture by gluing it to a piece of cardboard—or leave it unmounted.

VARIATION

1 Make a hanging using a colorful cardboard box. Do not paint the box, but use the colors already on it to make a new pattern.

2 Cut strips of cardboard and weave them together.

3 Attach a string to hang the pattern on the wall.

WEAVING PAPER HEARTS

In Denmark, people decorate Christmas trees with little woven hearts. To make the hearts successfully, you need to cut and measure accurately.

1 Choose two pieces of paper. Fold them in half so that the better side of the paper faces inward.

2 Make a card **template** like the one below.

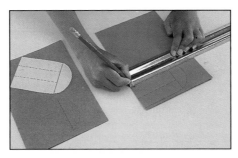

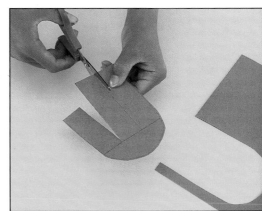

4 Cut out the shapes and along the "fingers" very carefully with scissors. Reverse the fold.

5 Weave the "fingers" of the two paper hearts in and out of each other. Do not cut anything.

3 Place the straight edge of the template on the fold of the first piece of paper. Trace the template. Then draw on the "fingers" accurately, using a ruler. Repeat this process with the second piece of paper.

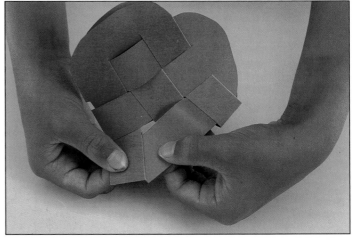

6 Make a handle. Either cut one out of paper, folded double, or use a piece of ribbon.

7 Fill the heart with sweets or tiny presents. Hang it on a tree or decorative branch.

8 Make both small and big hearts, with three, four, and five fingers. Use different sorts of paper. You can also use felt to make the hearts, and you can decorate them with embroidery.

IKAT WEAVING

In ikat weaving, the threads are dyed first so they will make a pattern when they are woven. The weaver has to make sure the warps and wefts are correctly positioned to produce the pattern in the cloth. Ikat is normally woven in narrow strips to help the weaver control the design. Even so, the different colors blur into each other, creating an unusual and beautiful effect.

Ikat is the name given to this technique in Indonesia, where it is very popular. However, people in many different parts of the world have used the same idea.

To do your own ikat weaving, you will need to use dyes. Cold-water dyes are cheap and easy to use. You can buy them at an arts and crafts store. Follow the instructions on the package. Dyes can be very messy. Always wear an apron and rubber gloves. Put down old newspapers to protect surfaces.

1 From a ball of thin cotton string, cut off 20 lengths, each two yards long.

2 Put them in a dye bath of a light color, perhaps a lemon yellow or a light orange. Leave for an hour. Rinse and let dry.

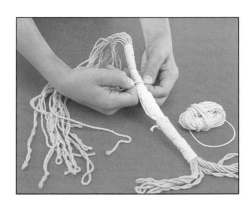

3 Fold the lengths in half. Decide which parts of the string will stay the first color. Wrap these areas in plastic wrap and bind them tightly with string.

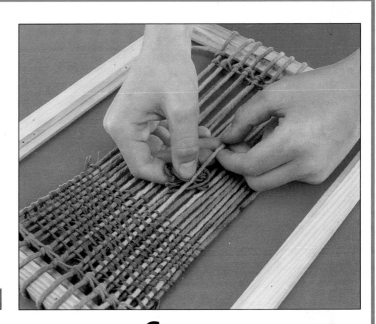

4 Put the string in a dye bath of a slightly darker color, perhaps a red or a light blue. The dye will not color the wrapped areas. Soak for an hour, rinse, and let dry.

5 Use a plain warp and your dyed string as the weft. Push the weft down with a comb so that it covers the warp.

6 Or use the dyed string as the warp and a plain weft of another color. Do *not* push the weft down to cover the warp.

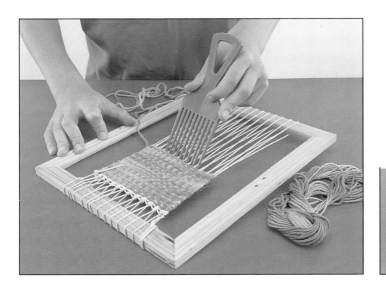

GETTING A MESSAGE ACROSS

Weaving can be used to give information or a message to other people. For example, you could make a tapestry to celebrate a special or historic event—a holiday, a vacation, or a great storm. Or you might want to make a piece protesting something that worries or upsets you; for example, cruelty to animals or litter. You can do this by weaving carefully chosen pictures, or **symbols**, into the tapestry, or by including found objects that have a special meaning.

If you are going to include a lot of found objects, it may be easier to make the piece without using a loom.

1 Find a length of wood or metal to use as a warp holder. It must not be able to bend. Make sure it looks good, as it will be part of the finished piece. A tree branch, a broom handle, a piece of driftwood, a dowel, or a wooden coat hanger with a trouser bar would be excellent. A wire coat hanger is not suitable.

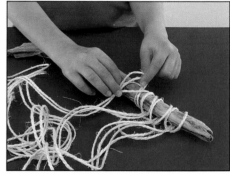

2 Cut lengths of string, twice the length of the warp you need.

3 Fold the warp threads in half and attach them to the warp holder using a double hitch knot (see page 17).

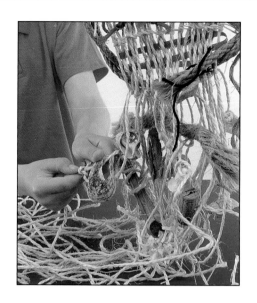

4 Hang the holder at a comfortable working height by attaching some string or screwing a hook in to the warp holder.

5 Weave in the weft and the found objects. Make sure the found objects are held firmly in place by several rows of weft above and below.

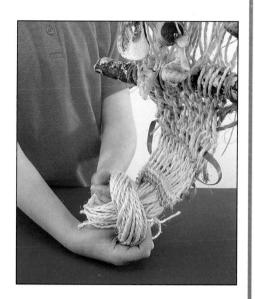

6 When you reach the bottom of your weaving, group the warp threads all together, or into threes or fours, and knot them firmly. Alternatively, experiment with braiding the ends together, or leaving some to hang free.

THE GALLERY

Find ideas for your weavings in all kinds of places. You might find some good ideas for a weaving by illustrating part of a story that you have written or enjoyed reading. Sometimes several weavings are made to tell different parts of a story.

Weaving is a good way to explore color, shape, and texture. Look around you. Look for things that have **contrasting** colors. Try to find patterns that could be simplified into a network of crisscrossing lines. Take photographs, collect postcards, or cut out pictures from magazines. These pictures will give you some ideas.

▲ *Rolling hills.*

◄ *A glass building.*

▼ *Rushing water.*

▲ *A patterned, tiled roof.*

A painting by Mark Rothko. ▶

▲ *The nest of a weaver bird.*

A dew-covered spider's web. ▶

▼ *Colorful houses.*

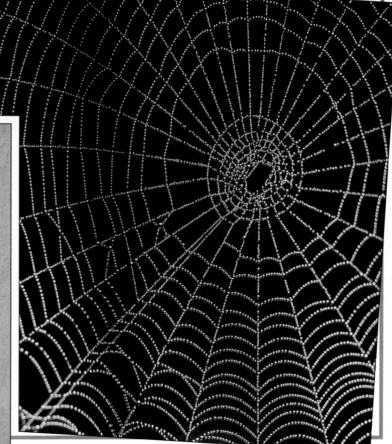

DESIGNING FOR WEAVING

Think of a weaving as being based on a grid made up of horizontal and vertical lines. In this way, adapt patterns or pictures to make a design for weaving.

2 Make a full-sized drawing of your chosen design, marking in the colors and materials that you will use. This sort of drawing is known as a cartoon. It can be attached behind the warp, to be a guide as you weave.

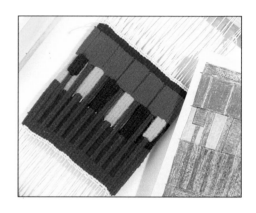

1 Make some sketches of designs. Decide which you like best.

3 Some of the most successful weavings use bold, simple shapes. You can weave curved and **diagonal** lines, but this will need careful planning. To weave a very smooth curve you will need to use fine warps and wefts, and the weaving will take a long time. Remember this when you are planning the project.

CHANGING COLOR

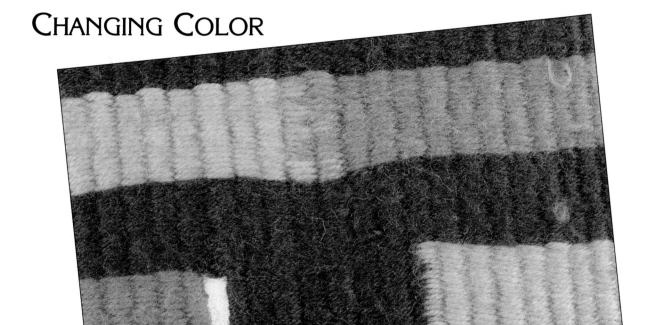

To introduce different colors in the weft, weave along the warp to a certain point, then double back in the opposite direction. This can be done in three ways.

1 Comb-dovetailing: Turn back the weft, first from one side and then the other, over a common warp.

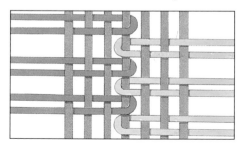

▲ Three ways of changing color: teething (top); slits (left); comb-dovetailing (right).

2 Teething: Turn back the wefts from either side over two warps that lie next to each other. Alternate the wefts over first one and then the other warp.

3 Slits: Turn back the wefts from either side over two warps that lie next to each other. This will leave a hole.

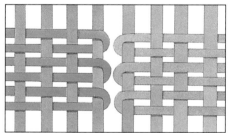

Any loose ends of the weft can be sewn in neatly at the back of the weaving, using a tapestry needle.

GLOSSARY

Abstract Not like real objects.

Ancient Greeks The people who lived in Greece about 2,000 years ago.

Archaeologists People who find out what happened in the past by studying ancient remains.

Bodkin A big, blunt sewing needle with a very large eyehole.

Cartoon The special name given to a full-sized, accurate plan for a piece of craftwork.

Chemicals Substances that react with each other to form different substances. They are used to make artificial fabrics, toiletries, medicines, and hundreds of other things.

Commissioned Specially ordered.

Contrasting Things contrast when they are very unlike one another. Black and white are contrasts.

Diagonal Slanting.

Engineered Made very precisely to exact measurements.

Felting A method of making cloth from woolen fibers. Wool has tiny hooks on each fiber. When the fibers are moistened and rubbed the hooks mesh together to form the cloth.

Fibers The tiny threads used to make cloth.

Grid A network of crisscrossing lines.

Horizontal Going across; the opposite of vertical. The horizon is horizontal.

Industrial Revolution The changes that took place in Western Europe and the United States during the eighteenth and nineteenth centuries. Factories were built to produce goods in large amounts. Many people stopped working on farms and went to work in the factories.

Interlaced Joined together by crossing, particularly by weaving.

Knitting A method of making cloth from yarn. Two long needles are used for knitting by hand.

Legend An ancient story that is told over and over until people believe it is true even though they can't prove it.

Middle Ages A period of history in Europe from about A.D. 1000 to the fifteenth century. Objects and events from this period are called medieval.

Nomadic Nomads are people who constantly travel from place to place, usually to look for grass to feed their animals. They have a nomadic lifestyle.

Parallel lines Straight lines that are always the same distance from one another and never meet.

Pharaoh The name given to the kings of ancient Egypt.

Preserved Protected so as not to decay over a period of time.

Rigid Stiff, unbending.

Shuttle A tool used in weaving to make it easier to pass the weft over and under the warp. It is usually a narrow strip of wood, with a notch at each end, over which the weft is wound.

Symbols Signs or pictures that are used to mean something else. In art, symbols are used to get across an idea or a message.

Tapestry Cloth that is woven on a frame, or embroidery done on a piece of canvas. This book looks only at woven tapestries.

Taut Tight; the opposite of slack or loose.
Techniques Methods or skills.
Template A shape cut out of something stiff, such as cardboard, that can be traced over and over.
Tension Tightness; the amount that something has been stretched or pulled.
Textile Any kind of fabric or cloth.
Texture The surface of a material.

Three-dimensional Having depth as well as height and width.
Treadle A foot pedal for working a machine.
Vertical Going up and down; the opposite of horizontal. A lightpole is vertical.
Weights Heavy objects used to pull or press something down.

FURTHER INFORMATION

BOOKS TO READ

Lancaster, John. *Fabric Art* (New York: Franklin Watts, 1991).

Patterson, Geoffrey. *Story of Wool* (North Pomfret, Vt.: Trafalgar, 1988).

Smith, Elizabeth S. *Cloth: Inventions That Changed Our Lives* (New York: Walker & Co., 1985).

Whyman, Kathryn. *Textiles* (New York: Franklin Watts, 1988).

SUPPLIERS

Some suppliers of materials for weaving are listed below. Also check the Yellow Pages in the telephone directory.

Cotton Clouds
Route 2
Safford, AZ 85546

Glimakra Looms 'n Yarns, Inc.
1338 Ross Street
Petaluma, CA 94954

Rio Grande Weaver's Supply
216 North Pueblo Road
Taos, NM 97571

The Batik and Weaving Supplier
393 Massachuesetts Avenue
Arlington, MA 02174

The Weaver's Shop & Yarn Co.
39 Courtland, Box 473
Rockford, MI 49341

Weaving Works
4717 Brooklyn Avenue, N.E.
Seattle, WA 98105

For further information about arts and crafts, contact the following organization:

The American Craft Council
72 Spring Street
New York, NY 10012

INDEX

ACKNOWLEDGMENTS

The publishers would like to thank the following for allowing their photographs to be reproduced: Bridgeman Art Library 7 (both), 27 top right; British Museum 6 top; Bruce Coleman Limited 27 center left (C. Fredriksson); Crafts Council 10 top right and bottom left, 11 left; David Cripps 11 right; Eye Ubiquitous 9 bottom (T. Brown), 26 bottom right (R. Friend); Michael Holford 6 bottom; Hutchison Library 8 top right (B. Regent), 8 bottom; Sharon Marcus 10 bottom right; Photri 9 top left; Sheffield City Art Galleries 4 right (D. Greaves); South American Pictures title page, 5, 8 top left; Tony Stone Worldwide 26 left, 27 top left (M. Busselle), 27 bottom right (B. Blauser); Zefa 4 left, 9 top right, 26 top (W. Thompson), 27 bottom left. All other photographs, including cover, were supplied by Zul Mukhida. Logo artwork and artwork on page 29 was supplied by John Yates.

The tapestry weaving on page 4 was designed by pupils from Myrtle Springs School, Sheffield, England.

The painting by Mark Rothko on page 27 appears by permission of the copyright holders: © 1992 Kate Rothke-Prizel & Christopher Rothke/ARS, N.Y. The tapestry *The Labours of the Months* (page 7 top) and the William Morris tapestry *Cabbage and Vine* (page 7 bottom) both appear by courtesy of The Board of Trustees of the Victoria and Albert Museum.